Dracula:
The Real Story

Ken Derby

Copyright © 2014 by Kenneth Derby

All rights reserved.

Illusion Publishing
www.illusionpublishing.me
First Published in 2014

ISBN-10: 0615919758
ISBN-13: 978-0615919751

Cover designed by Najla Qamber Designs (www.najlaqamberdesigns.com)

Illustration by Harry Wilson
(http://harry-the-fox.deviantart.com)

Formatting by Polgarus Studio
(www.polgarusstudio.com)

Acknowledgments

I give special thanks to the late Nicolae Paduraru, former president of the Transylvanian Society of Dracula, based in Bucharest. Thanks, Nick, for the wonderful insider tour of Vlad's Romania and for checking the historical accuracy of my manuscript. You are sorely missed.

I thank the Transylvanian Society of Dracula for their support during this project.

I thank Dr. Constantin Rezachevici, chief researcher at the Institute of History Nicolae Iorga (in Bucharest), for his insights concerning the Order of the Dragon. I also thank the Institute for finalizing bits and pieces of history about Dracula and for providing me with maps of Valahia and Europe.

I also thank Dr. Elizabeth Miller, professor of English at the Memorial University of Newfoundland, for reviewing my manuscript and for being so generous in sharing her views and research with me about the Bram Stoker/Vlad Dracula connection.

And finally, I thank Bram Stoker for giving us Count Dracula. What would the world be without the bloodsucking fiend terrorizing our lives on page and on film?

From Jonathan Harker's Journal in *Dracula*:
"Buda-Pesth seems a wonderful place…"
And that it is!

Ken Derby
Budapest

In Memory of Nicolae Padararu

"A narrative that retains its crispness without sacrificing its moments of drama, this biography provides a balanced and accurate overview of Vlad the Impaler (Dracula), and is an excellent resource for young students."
—DR. ELIZABETH MILLER, President of the Canadian Chapter of the Transylvanian Society of Dracula

Contents

Acknowledgments iii
Prologue 1
A Prince? 5
Son of the Dragon 7
Abandoned 13
The Assassination 17
Freedom 21
The Fall 25
Revenge 27
Castle Dracula-Poenari 33
The Trail of Terror 37
The Impaler vs. The Conqueror 43
The Fall of Castle Dracula-Poenari 53
Double-Crossed 57
Freedom 61
Another Assassination 65
Epilogue 69
About the Author 71
A Note From the Author 73
Maps 75
Glossary of Important Historical Figures 79
Research Sources 83
Links 85
Other Books by Ken Derby 87

Prologue

A Quiz: Who Was the Real Dracula? Dracula #1 or Dracula #2?

Dracula #1

Blood trickled down the young woman's smooth neck and over her bare shoulder. A tall, thin man dressed in black ran his tongue over his lips as he stared at the crimson stain blossoming on the front of the woman's white nightgown. To continue his feast, the count slid his hand behind her delicate neck and forced her head back.

Four men burst into the moonlit room, and the count turned to face the intruders. His eyes burned as red as his victim's blood, and his nostrils flared. He hissed a primal, animalistic warning at the foursome. Blood dripped from his razor-sharp teeth as his lips parted into a devilish grin. With catlike speed, he tossed the half-drained girl on the bed like a ragdoll, then sprang eagerly at the men, showing no fear whatsoever.

The would-be rescuers thrust crucifixes into the face of the bloodthirsty count, and the religious relics sent him backpedaling to the other side of the room, where he cowered like a cornered animal. A black cloud blew across the moon, casting a distinct and timely darkness over the room and everyone in it. Within seconds a gas lamp, lit by one of the rescuers, cast fingers of light into the far corners of the room.

But the count was nowhere to be seen; all that was left in his wake was a trail of gray mist that snaked under the door and out of the room.

And so, the count lived on to feed on the blood of others.[1]

Dracula #2

Blood trickled and then streamed down the man's forehead and neck with each swing of the hammer. The metal-on-metal *clang*, combined with wails of anguish, echoed off the castle walls. A short, stocky man dressed in black paused to relish the moment. He stroked his long, curled mustache and gazed into the terror-filled eyes of his latest victim. Not one to waste precious time, he positioned another nail against the head of the man, raised his hammer, and finished his bloody task.

Earlier, a small contingent of Italian ambassadors had arrived at the castle to visit the prince. Upon arrival, they had taken off their hats and hoods, but left their skullcaps in place as they bowed before their royal host. The prince, obviously annoyed, asked why they hadn't also removed their skullcaps in his presence.

The ambassadors explained that it was the custom of Italians; they would not remove their skullcaps for anyone,

---

[1] Adapted from Bram Stoker's *Dracula* (first published in 1887)

not even for the Sultan of the Ottoman Empire or for the Holy Roman Emperor himself. The prince then announced that it would be an honor to strengthen and recognize their customs. The ambassadors immediately bowed to the prince, praised his greatness, and thanked him for his understanding, not realizing who they were dealing with and what lay in store for them.

The prince declared that he would recognize their customs in a way they would never forget, and within minutes, he and his personal guards seized the ambassadors. Surprised and too afraid to fight back, the ambassadors crumpled to the floor and begged for mercy. The prince chuckled as he cruelly nailed the skullcaps onto their heads and then sent them back to Italy.

And the prince lived on to terrorize the lives of others.[2]

> Once again: Who was the real Dracula?
> Was it Dracula #1, the count?
> Or Dracula #2, the prince?
> The answer is: Dracula #2, the prince!

---

[2] Adapted from German meistersinger Michael Beheim's narrative, first written in the mid-1400s and later chronicled in *Dracula: Prince of Many Faces* (Published in 1989)

A Prince?

Dracula, a prince? I don't think so, you might say to yourself. Princes are noble, charming, and civilized. Besides, I've never heard of this skull-nailing, bloody carpenter. Dracula's a bloodsucker, a vampire, right? Fangs, blood, bats, garlic, wooden stakes, castles, Transylvania...you know—the count!

Ah, yes. The count. The world knows about him, but where did he come from? The truth is that he was conjured up in the world of fiction, penned out of the imaginings of Irish author Bram Stoker. *Dracula*, Stoker's classic horror masterpiece published in 1897, is a romantic and terror-filled tale set in Transylvania and England. The story includes a creepy castle, coffins, a spider-eating madman, vampire hunters, and the most famous bloodsucker of all time, Count Dracula.

Today, vampire novels, films, and television shows seem to be in vogue, with several variations, from long-haired, contemporary bloodsuckers lurking around historical New Orleans to attractive teen vamps struggling with romance and life, but while few realize it, *Dracula* was not the first vampire novel of its time. It is likely that Stoker was influenced by *The Vampyr* (1819), written by John Polidori, and by Joseph Sheridan Le Fanu's *Carmilla* (1872). Mary Shelley's famous novel, *Frankenstein* (1818), might have also played an inspirational role in Stoker's nightmarish publication.

Bram Stoker had been planning to write a vampire novel even before he came across the count's infamous name. In fact, he originally intended to name the world's most famous vampire Count Wampyr. But in the summer of 1890, Stoker, a reader who frequented the Whitby Public Library, discovered a book by William Wilkinson that made reference to Dracula, a prince who ruled a Romanian province during the mid-1400s. After reading Wilkinson's *An Account of the Principalities of Wallachia and Moldavia*, Stoker not only changed the name of his vampire but later the name of the novel itself to *Dracula*.

Other books and articles also provided Stoker with many fascinating facts about the prince's native Romania, which raises a question. Did Prince Dracula's shadowy life, intertwined with and inseparable from the complex politics of fifteenth-century Europe, inspire Stoker as he molded the fictional character of Count Dracula? It is not possible to answer this question, as there is no documentation to support this idea. However, it is interesting to note that as well as exceptional intelligence and a grim disposition, the count exhibits extraordinary power, arrogance, and barbarity in *Dracula*. It is most likely a coincidence that these remarkable traits were also displayed in the personality and life of the real Dracula, but even so, it is a strange coincidence.

Son of the Dragon

The real Dracula was born in Transylvania ("beyond the forest"), a section of Romania, in December of 1431. Since ancient times, this beautiful land of forests and mountains has been inhabited by Daco-Romans, Romanians.

When Dracula was born, Transylvania was a part of Europe, an empire that stretched from the Atlantic Ocean to the northwest corner of the Black Sea; for the most part Europe was a single civilization. During this time in history, Europe was dealing with a serious, seemingly insurmountable problem, the Ottoman Empire, which had extended from the southern shores of the Black Sea to the waters of the Aegean Sea. The powerful Ottoman Turks had one thing in mind: to expand their Empire and conquer Europe at all costs.

In February of 1431, several months prior to Dracula's birth, Europe had no choice but to face the Turks. Twenty-four members of European royalty met in Nuremberg, Germany. These twenty-four men were members of The Order of the Dragon, a society established in 1408 by Sigismund of Luxembourg.

Dracula's father, Vlad, was invited to join the society because Valahia[3], his homeland just to the south of Transylvania, was strategically located along the Danube and acted as a buffer between the Turks and Europe. Vlad traveled to Nuremberg and joined the coalition at a special induction ceremony. The society had many objectives, but its main goal was to protect the very life of King Sigismund. The Order of the Dragon also resolved to defend the Christian Empire against the advancing Islamic Turks. Knights of the society were identified by the green or red capes they wore during special ceremonies. A gold medallion engraved with a dragon and a cross was worn at all times by knights of the society.

Vlad swore his allegiance to the European Empire at the ceremony, and The Order agreed to appoint him prince of Valahia, a nation that was ruled, at the time, by Alexandru Aldea, his half-brother. However, with his own personal agenda in mind, King Sigismund overruled The Order of the Dragon, and Aldea remained on the throne. In lieu of princely duties, Vlad was granted the title of military governor of Transylvania.

When Vlad returned to Transylvania, he began to be known as Dracul, which means "dragon" and "devil" in the Romanian language. Upper-class citizens who knew of his membership in The Order of the Dragon referred to him as Dracul the Dragon because of the pledge he'd taken to help protect the European Empire. Common citizens who

---

[3] *Valahia* is the proper Romanian word for Vlad's homeland. However, the word *Wallachia* has been used in Western publications for many years.

knew nothing of his secret membership in The Order simply called him Dracul the Devil. This was not because he was an evil man; rather, the image of a dragon also represented the devil.

Dracul's main job as governor was to guard the border between Valahia and Transylvania. The Turks, with Aldea's support, had established a base in the Danube port town of Giurgiu. That base, as well as Aldea's association with the Turks, was of primary concern to the European Empire.

In the spring of 1431, Dracul established his headquarters in Sighisoara, a hillside fortress that stood guard over central Transylvania. Fourteen massive battle towers and thick walls made of stone and brick surrounded Sighisoara, and even the powerful cannons of the Turks could cause little damage to the structure. Dracul was confident that Sighisoara would be a safe haven to work from.

In the latter part of 1431, Vlad Dracula ("son of the dragon"), Dracul's second son, was born in a enormous three-story stone house on the main square of Sighisoara, just a stone's throw away from the impressive clock tower. Dracula's older brother, Mircea, was three at the time.

The two boys' early childhoods were dominated by the women of the household: their mother, midwives, and wet nurses. The women of that era had two main tasks: to teach the boys how to behave like royalty and also to instruct them in three languages, Hungarian, Latin, and German. It was assumed that the boys would one day hold leadership positions within the empire, so a proper upbringing was essential.

Like other boys at that time, Dracula and his brother no doubt enjoyed playing in and about the numerous alleyways that branched off the busy town square. The alleyways, lined with uneven cobblestone, led to many mysterious stairways that snaked between dark buildings. The stairways ran up and down the hillside, perfect for curious, energetic young explorers. When time allowed between their lessons, the boys could work their way through the labyrinth of alleyways and stairs that would take them to the creepy cemetery that loomed above the fortress.

Dracula most definitely enjoyed feast days, when the town square took on a different look altogether. Acrobats performed death-defying acts to the delight of all. Children and adults stood side by side and were entertained by Biblical puppet shows. Artists advanced through the square and sketched funny caricatures of various characters in the noisy crowd. The melodies of singers and musicians, perched upon wagons and carts, drifted out over the square, adding to the boisterous celebration. Much drink, food, and fun were the order of such days.

Summer signaled the start of games and running and jumping contests. Many-a-summer's day was spent horseback riding, and by five years of age, Dracula was able to ride an unsaddled horse at full gallop. In the winter, Mircea practiced shooting his bow and arrows, hunted eagles with his slingshot, and trapped rabbits, and young Dracula tagged along whenever possible. When the snow came, they spent as much time possible sledding down the steep hills in and around Sighisoara.

But life was not all fun and games for anyone living at that time. Physical endurance was of utmost importance during the 1400s, and one had to be strong to survive. The boys were often forced to brave blizzards and rainstorms with little clothing to keep them warm; they were never coddled, and it was hoped that such treatment would strengthen their physical and moral character. After all, it was never too early to begin preparation for the roles they would play in adulthood, when they would be royal warriors.

Abandoned

Mircea and young Vlad Dracula had a great role model to follow in their father, a true warrior. In 1436, Dracul learned that Alexandru Aldea was near death, so he decided the time was right to advance upon Valahia, hoping to seize the throne. His army, aided by the use of cannons, gained the upper hand in a number of small battles against the Turks. Then, in December of 1436, Dracul led his troops into Tirgoviste, the capital of Valahia. He stormed the palace, overthrew Aldea, and became prince of Valahia. A few months later, his wife and three sons, Mircea, Vlad Dracula, and Radu (born in 1435), joined him in Tirgoviste.

Young Vlad Dracula's life changed a great deal as soon as he arrived in Tirgoviste. Life became more serious, and there was less time for play. Between the ages of five and eleven, he was taught swimming, fencing, jousting, archery, advanced horsemanship, and proper manners. Dracula didn't attend school, but he had several private tutors who taught him Latin, Italian, and a small amount of French and Hungarian. He also studied mathematics, world history, political science, and the humanities.

Unfortunately young Dracula's studies were interrupted in 1442 by a devious scheme organized by Sultan Murad II, ruler of the Turks. The sultan invited Dracul to his court to discuss regional politics. Dracul, thinking the meeting was a wise idea, agreed to visit the sultan in the Bulgarian city of Gallipoli. He took two of his sons, Dracula and his younger brother, Radu, on the journey, as he thought the trip would be exciting for the boys.

And exciting it was! Turkish troops arrested Dracul at the Gallipoli city gates, accused him of disloyalty, and disappeared with him into the heart of the city. Dracul's two young sons were spirited away to a remote mountain fortress in Egrigöz in Asia Minor.

A year after his arrest, Dracul struck a deal with the sultan and was released: He promised not to take any further action against Turkish interests upon reclaiming the throne from Mircea, who had been ruling since his father's arrest. To prove his loyalty, Dracul left Dracula and Radu, his own flesh and blood, in Turkish hands, as a guarantee that he would honor his pact. Then, without his two youngest sons, Dracul returned to Valahia.

Dracula, eleven, and Radu, only seven, suddenly found themselves alone in a strange land, surrounded by people who spoke a language they did not understand. The feeling of abandonment must have weighed heavily on the boys' hearts; after all, their own father had left them behind.

Both boys were later taken to Adrianople, the capital of the Ottoman Empire. There, they were fathered and educated by the best Ottoman tutors, and both became fluent in the Turkish language.

In spite of their shared bloodline, the two brothers were as different as night and day. Dracula, a somewhat ugly child, was a difficult student with a bad temper. His tutors didn't hesitate to use the whip on him when necessary, and when that didn't work, they employed even harsher forms of punishment. During his long stay with the Turks, young Dracula experienced torture and terror firsthand, and distrust and revenge became a part of his very soul.

Radu, on the other hand, a very handsome boy and an obedient student—obviously the favorite of the two—received special treatment from his captors. He was also quite popular with the young ladies and the minions of the sultan's court. Eventually, Radu the Handsome, as he would later be called, won the favor of the sultan and became a member of his court.

During their years of captivity, the brotherly love between Dracula and Radu developed into a blazing-hot hatred, jealousy, and bitterness that poisoned their relationship for the remainder of their lives.

The Assassination

Meanwhile, back in Valahia, Dracul found himself in an uncomfortable position. As a member of The Order of the Dragon, he was obliged to support the European Empire's crusades against the Turks. However, he had recently promised the sultan, by swearing on both the Bible and the Koran, that he would not take up arms against the Ottoman Empire. Attempting to maintain the independence of Valahia was difficult amidst the complex and confusing politics of the day.

Fearing the worst for his young sons, who were still held hostage by the Turks, Dracul convinced his eldest, Mircea, to participate with him in several campaigns against the Turks in 1445. He worried what would happen to his sons as a result of breaking his pact, and he feared the sultan would torture or even behead them. Dracul anticipated the worst and wrote the following about his boys: "Please understand that I have allowed my children to be butchered for the sake of Christian peace, in order that I and my country might continue to be vassals to the Holy Roman Empire."

A shrewd politician and strategist, Dracul managed to play both sides of the fence by frequently switching loyalty between the European and the Ottoman Empires. In the summer of 1447, when he learned that the sultan had spared his sons, he signed a peace treaty with the Turks. This act greatly angered the Europeans and prompted John Hunyadi, viceroy of Hungary and powerful leader of the European crusades against the Turks, to take action against Dracul. In December of 1447, Hunyadi enlisted the help of Vladislav II (from the Danesti family, a rival of Dracul's living in Transylvania) and crossed the rugged Carpathian Mountains into Valahia. They had one goal in mind: to murder Dracul.

Vladislav sent spies ahead to Tirgoviste; their mission was to infiltrate the city and stir up unrest among Dracul's political enemies. As Hunyadi and Vladislav advanced upon Tirgoviste, Dracul and Mircea closed the city gates, but it was too little too late, for Vladislav's spies were already within the city walls, stirring up trouble among Tirgoviste's citizens, mainly the boyars, the wealthy aristocrats of the society. The boyars owned or controlled immense estates that often included several villages; each estate was ruled by a great boyar, a governor, and these lords of the land wielded a surprising amount of power.

It wasn't long before violent unrest broke out among the boyars, and that violence was directed at Dracul and Mircea. They had no choice but to take up arms to defend themselves.

The rioting raged on, and the boyars closed in on Dracul and Mircea. Dracul and Mircea fought for their lives, but their enemies overwhelmed them. Eventually, the boyars captured Mircea. Showing no mercy whatsoever, they blinded Dracul's oldest child with red-hot iron stakes, then buried him alive.

Dracul was able to slip out of Tirgoviste under the cover of darkness. He hoped to reach friendly Turkish troops that he knew were camped on the Danube River, but he only made it as far as the marshes of Baleteni, where he was overtaken and assassinated by Vladislav and the boyars. Later, Dracul's supporters gathered his body off the mist-shrouded marsh and buried it in a small wooden chapel near Tirgoviste.

Then, just like that, Vladislav became ruler of Valahia.

Freedom

Sultan Murad II informed Dracula of his father's and brother's murders at the end of 1447. Even though Dracula's father had abandoned him, the loss he felt must have been heartbreaking, and the sultan's grim news planted a bad seed in Dracula's heart, the seed of revenge.

While Dracula was not the favorite, the sultan was impressed with his strong will and cunning personality, so much so that when Dracula was twenty, he was granted freedom. The Turks, unhappy that Vladislav II had gained the throne of Valahia, realized that Dracula was the right man for the throne.

A cavalry of Turkish soldiers, led by Dracula, stormed into Valahia and captured the throne in 1448. Unfortunately, his Turkish support dwindled, and Dracula worried about his father's assassins, wondering if they would come after him as well. He also worried that Vladislav II, with the help of Hunyadi, might attempt to recapture Valahia. Uncertain and fretting about his position on the throne and even his very life, Dracula fled to Moldavia. There, his short-lived reign ended after two short months, and Vladislav II once again became ruler of Valahia.

Dracula lived in Moldavia from December 1449 until October 1451. Much of his time was spent with his cousin, Stephen. The two became close friends and made a pact that they would support each other, with force if necessary, whenever either of them needed help in securing their thrones.

Stephen's father was assassinated in October of 1451. Stephen and Vlad, fearing for their lives, slipped out of Moldavia and journeyed through Borgo Pass into Transylvania. Historians are not sure why Dracula made such a brash move; by entering Transylvania, he placed himself in the hands of the very man who had ordered his father's assassination, John Hunyadi.

Dracula went into hiding somewhere near the city of Brasov, and he immediately began to plan and organize an attack on Vladislav. Humiliated and angry, he was desperate to reign over Valahia once again. When word leaked out that Dracula was back in the neighborhood, Vladislav and Hunyadi sent letters of protest to the mayor of Brasov, instructing him to run Dracula out of the country.

When Dracula learned that Vladislav and Hunyadi were aware of his whereabouts, he decided to flee to the nearby city of Sibiu. Hunyadi heard about Dracula's plans and immediately hired an assassin to ambush him in the village of Gioagiu, but Dracula learned of the ambush beforehand and was able to avoid the assassination attempt.

As infuriating as it was for Hunyadi, Dracula's escape was the least of his worries. The Ottomans had crowned a new sultan, Mehmed II, after Murad II, his father, died of a stroke on February 3, 1451. Mehmed, full of ambition, had his eyes on Constantinople, strategically situated at the entrance to the Black Sea. Lying both in Europe and Asia, the Black Sea was the eastern cornerstone of the Christian Empire, and it had been since the year 330. Mehmed's desire to conquer Constantinople was cause for alarm for all of Christian Europe.

To make matters even worse, Vladislav II had adopted a pro-Turkish policy, and this made Hunyadi uneasy. Considering the fragile state of Europe, Hunyadi realized only one person could replace Vladislav on the Valahian throne and hopefully help save the empire, and that man was Dracula. After all, Dracula had lived much of his tumultuous life in Turkey, so he spoke Turkish and was aware of their military tactics. Not only that, but he'd grown up with Mehmed, and he knew what made the man's mind tick.

The two enemies met in Hunyadi's lofty palace that was perched on a huge rock outside of Hunedoara. Spurred on by their hate for a common enemy, they laid their history aside for a time and agreed to form an alliance. Dracula was granted a position in Hunyadi's army. This was very beneficial to Dracula, because Hunyadi, one of the top military commanders of the day, taught Dracula important tactics and battle strategies that he would later employ. It is also important to note that Emperor Sigismund, the king of Hungary, agreed to Dracula's appointment and commissioned him to guard the Transylvanian border against Turkish attacks, much like his father had done several years before.

The Fall

On May 29, 1453, the dreaded event occurred: Turkish troops attacked Constantinople. Mercenaries, foot soldiers, elite troops, and even the sultan's bodyguards scaled the walls and stormed the city.

Three days later, Mehmed entered the city gates, sitting high and proud upon his steed, and found that his troops had brought the war-torn city to its knees. Mehmed wasted no time and directed his steed to St. Sophia's Cathedral. Upon entering the holy cathedral, he knelt and bowed toward Mecca and recited the following prayer: "There is no God but Allah, and Mohammed is His Prophet." Since that day, Constantinople has been a Muslim city.

When all was said and done, 4,000 people were killed and 50,000 captured, including men, women, and children of all ages. The news of events in Constantinople shocked Christian Europe, and all Europeans found it difficult to accept that the Ottomans now reigned on their continent. Fear gripped hearts at the realization that Serbia, Bulgaria, and the Byzantine Empire lay in Turkish hands. They wondered what the Ottomans would take next, if it would be Valahia, Transylvania, Hungary, or all of Europe. An Ottoman advance was likely, but they had no idea when it would occur. Certainly, the situation seemed bleak for the European Empire.

In the summer of 1456, the plague reared its ugly head, a horrible disease that stole the lives of men, women, children, and even infants. Not even those in power were immune, and on August 11 of that year, the sickness did what no enemy had ever managed to do: It took the life of John Hunyadi. The loss of the great military leader was a bad turn of fate for the Christian cause, and to make matters even worse, Vladislav II had formed an alliance with the Turks, which gave them an open door into Europe.

While Hunyadi was on his deathbed, waiting for the plague to end his life, Dracula and a hodgepodge of mercenaries swooped out of the Carpathian Mountains into Valahia. Outside of Tirgoviste, they confronted Vladislav's troops and immediately attacked them.

Dracula, caught up in the excitement, threw himself into the raging battle. With vengeance for the murder of his father and brother coursing through his veins, he fought his way through the skirmish. He soon found himself face to face with Vladislav. The two mortal enemies charged each other, knowing full well that only one of them would be alive when the struggle was over. As the din of battle died down, only one man was left standing, and that man was Dracula.

Revenge

In August of 1456, at the age of twenty-five, Dracula seized the throne of Valahia once again. He quickly became an imposing figure, and his strength of mind and soul was reflected in his appearance. Niccoló Modrussa, papal legate to Buda, described Dracula this way:

He was not very tall but very stocky and strong, with a cold and terrible appearance, a strong and aquiline nose, swollen nostrils, a thin and reddish face in which the very long eyelashes framed large, wide-open green eyes; the bushy black eyebrows made them appear threatening. His face and chin were shaven, but for a mustache. The swollen temples increased the bulk of his head. A bull's neck connected with his head from which black, curly locks hung on his wide-shouldered person.[4]

In an elaborate ceremony in Tirgoviste, this young man with daunting physical features became: Prince Vlad, son of Vlad the Great, sovereign and ruler of Ungro-Valahia and of the duchies of Amlas and Fagaras.

Tirgoviste, the capital city, was located at the foot of the majestic Carpathian Mountains. Pristine lakes, connected by canals and filled with trout, surrounded the city and

---

[4] From *Dracula: Prince of Many Faces* (Published in 1989)

extended several miles into the countryside. A moat and walls circled the city, providing needed protection against enemies. Numerous businesses, palaces, and hundreds of simple homes cramped the inner city, and since space was so limited, many buildings spilled outside the city walls. Tirgoviste was a social and cultural center, as well as the seat of power.

It was from Tirgoviste that Dracula made many decisions as ruler of Valahia. Within the first few months of his reign, he made a very interesting political move: He swore his allegiance to both the Hungarians and the Turks! He was a cagey politician, much like his father, and he knew that playing both sides of the fence was essential if he was to retain his throne. Being a buffer and balancing policies between the European and Ottoman Empires was no easy task, but Dracula managed to do so in an extremely complicated political climate.

His thoughts about politics centered on power, as witnessed by a letter to the mayor of Brasov: "Pray, think that when a man or prince is powerful and strong at home, then he will be able to do as he wills. But when he is without power, another one more powerful than he will overwhelm him and do as he wishes."[5] Dracula's domination over others would prove to be advantageous in his role as prince of Valahia.

Stories and rumors about the murder of Dracula's older brother, Mircea, circulated throughout Tirgoviste. It was

---

[5] From *Dracula: Prince of Many Faces* (Published in 1989)

common knowledge that the boyars had been involved in the brutal assassination, but Dracula wasn't satisfied with stories. Because he wanted to see evidence of the crime with his own eyes, shortly after becoming prince, he ordered that his older brother's body be exhumed from the grave. Dracula found Mircea lying facedown in his coffin, his eye sockets charred and empty and his body twisted out of shape, as if he had been struggling to breathe after burial. The horrific sight confirmed the rumors: His brother had been cruelly blinded, then buried alive. Revenge once again burned in Dracula's heart, and he vowed that someone would someday pay for his brother's untimely and cruel death.

Payment came in the spring of 1457, when Dracula hosted a lavish Easter celebration in the meadows beyond the city walls. Several hundred boyars and merchants, along with their wives and children, lounged on carpets that were scattered about on the lush grass, enjoying a feast of roasted lamb, sweet cake, and wine.

When everyone's belly was full, the celebration turned into a festive affair. Gypsy musicians, minstrels, and jesters entertained the drunken adults, while the children stole away and played on swings and carousels. Groups of young men and women twirled, leapt, and kicked, dancing to the tunes of the gypsy bands. As evening drew near, laughter and merriment carried across the meadow and drifted off into the surrounding countryside.

All the while, Dracula stood aside, watching the festivities, knowing full well that his father's and brother's assassins were lurking somewhere amidst the happy throng before him. During the long winter, he'd meticulously planned a massive act of revenge, and to his pleasure, his plan was working perfectly; hundreds of drunken boyars were partying, without a clue as to why they had really been invited to the Easter celebration.

As the sun dipped behind the snowcapped mountains, Dracula nodded to one of his captains. Within seconds, the celebration came crashing to a halt as armed soldiers rushed the partiers from all sides of the meadow. Confusion and panic raced through the crowd as Dracula's soldiers arrested every person dressed in fancy, elaborate clothes, mainly boyars and wealthy merchants. The attack had come as such a surprise, at such an unexpected moment, that most were stunned and caught off guard, unable to escape.

Young boyars, wives, and children were chained together and forced into a makeshift stockade. From there, they witnessed Dracula's vengeful wrath. Screams of anguish pierced the calm night as the older boyars and merchants were impaled, one by one, in the very meadow where they'd just been eating, drinking, and making merry in the name of Easter.

Impalement was Dracula's favorite technique of execution. He tied the subject down, stretched his or her legs wide apart, then carefully hammered a round, oiled stake, about eight feet long, up the rectum; the stake was often driven in so far that it stuck out of the mouth of the victim. The unfortunate one was then raised aloft and left to die in agony, which sometimes took days of suffering. Dracula strictly forbade the removal of corpses from the stakes, and they were left to rot and were eventually eaten by birds.

Dracula's Easter massacre taught the remaining boyars a lesson they would never forget. From that day forward, any who did not submit to him would pay a hefty price. Not only was the massacre an act of revenge, but it was also an effective way to diminish the power of the meddling boyars so he could create a modern, centralized form of government.

Castle Dracula-Poenari

In time, Dracula began to feel that Tirgoviste was far too unstable and unpredictable to serve as a capital any longer, so he decided to rebuild an old castle that lay in ruins about fifty miles northwest. The old fortress, Castle Arges, sat high atop an imposing rock formation on a mountainside, above the Arges River. He believed that location, at the foot of the rugged Carpathian Mountains, would offer safe haven for his family, his treasures, and himself. He also had the necessary labor force in hand to rebuild the castle: the captured boyars.

The day after the Easter massacre, Dracula's soldiers marched the boyar prisoners, including women and children, northward, out of Tirgoviste. Chained together, the prisoners marched for two days over rugged terrain, to the village of Poenari. The walk was extremely demanding, and many died along the way.

The surviving boyars finally staggered into Poenari, their fine Easter clothes soiled and tattered from the ordeal. The peasants of Poenari gathered on the dusty street and stared at the unusual sight before them: Tirgoviste's subdued, battered, and confused elite.

Kilns had been built in the villages surrounding Castle Arges in preparation for the arrival of Dracula's captive workforce. During the long, hot summer, some of the captives were ordered to make bricks, while others formed human chains that stretched from numerous kilns to Castle Arges. They passed the heavy building materials from person to person, all the way up the rugged mountainside to the worksite. The captives were granted little food or rest, and any who dared to stop working, even due to fatigue, injury, or illness, were brutally beaten. The work was dangerous and difficult, and many boyars lost their lives, but the construction continued under Dracula's unforgiving guidance until the last brick was laid.

Castle Dracula-Poenari was small in comparison to other castles of the 1400s, but its design and location allowed it to serve as a reliable hideaway for Dracula and his family. Perched on a high, rocky cliff, it was secure against sneak attacks. The walls were doubled in thickness to withstand cannon fire. Five defensive towers ensured a clear view to the valley hundreds of feet below.

Dracula's Easter massacre and the hazards associated with the building of Castle Dracula-Poenari nearly wiped out the boyars. Revenge was Dracula's intention all along, and his new policies directed at the remaining boyars reflected his hatred of them. Without the least bit of concern, he confiscated boyar land and fortunes and passed them on to loyal peasants. He knew the peasants would see such a gesture as a godsend, and it would ensure peasant support and adoration in his revamped government.

As a result of Dracula's generosity, the peasants did indeed back Dracula and his policies. Over 90 percent of

Valahia's citizens were peasants, and uniting with them was instrumental to the success and longevity of Dracula's reign. Gaining the support of such a large segment of the population was a shrewd political move on Dracula's part, and the fact that most of the peasants were farmers appealed to him; he believed the agricultural skills and strong work ethic of the peasants would lead to a stronger country.

Even though Dracula had a strong following, he trusted very few individuals. In an effort to gain firsthand knowledge about the lives of his people, he often disguised himself and wandered about the villages, farms, and backwoods of Valahia, under the cover of darkness. If he discovered anything unacceptable, bloodshed would ensue. In fact, blood flowed all too often during Dracula's reign, a fact that might have inspired his modern-day, fictionalized reputation.

The Trail of Terror

For six years, Dracula terrorized his own people, the Roman Catholic Church, and the German merchants of Transylvania. A trail of terror seemed to always follow in his footsteps.

Revenge was the initial reason why Dracula embarked upon a life of terror. The assassinations of his father and brother greatly upset him, even though he'd been alienated by both during his youth. Dracula seemed to live his life by a Biblical code: "eye for an eye, a tooth for a tooth."[6] To provoke the wrath of Dracula was very dangerous indeed, a lesson Vladislav II and the boyars of Tirgoviste learned firsthand, albeit too late.

Some have described Dracula as the Romanian Robin Hood, a man who took from the rich (the boyars and merchants) and gave to the poor (the peasants). Many peasants benefited from his generosity, and many considered Dracula to be a national hero because he attempted to preserve the sovereignty of Valahia in very difficult times. However, it is also true that many of his own people greatly suffered directly from his violent acts of terror. He relied on terror for crime prevention, heaping it

---

[6] The Holy Bible, Exodus 21:24.

upon any untoward gypsies, beggars, and various rogues. Dracula himself said, "These men live off the sweat of others, so they are useless to humanity…may such men be eradicated from my land."[7]

One gypsy leader was found guilty of thievery and was promptly sentenced to death by Dracula. Knowing full well that he would soon be hanging from a stake, the gypsy protested and explained to Dracula that impalement was against the laws of his tribe. Dracula honored the gypsy's tribal laws, but he still took the leader's life through demented diplomacy. Rather than impaling the man, he boiled him alive in a big kettle of water. Then, to add further insult to the proceedings, he forced the tribe members to eat the flesh of their leader.

As cruel as he could be, Dracula also studied and dabbled in religion, mostly dominating the Romanian Orthodox faith and exploiting its influence to enhance his position within the land. He built many churches and monasteries and was often seen in the presence of Romanian Orthodox monks. The prince considered himself to be a Christian crusader, but it is doubtful that his belief in religious doctrine was strong. During his reign, the Roman Catholic faith spread into Valahia. Dracula was suspicious of the Catholics and feared their power and influence, a mistrust that led to many Catholic monasteries and monks experiencing the man's rage.

---

[7] From *Dracula: Prince of Many Faces* (Published in 1989)

One such event took place in Tirgoviste, when two monks visited Dracula in his palace. Ever the gracious but devious host, Dracula offered to give the monks a tour. The threesome made their way through the palace and eventually climbed to the top of Chindia Tower, the main tower overlooking the palace courtyard. The ghastly sight that met the monks' eyes horrified them, but neither said a word as they stared at the rotting, impaled bodies that littered the courtyard. One monk finally broke the silence and cautiously declared that Dracula had been appointed by God to punish evildoers. That cowardly monk lived to see the light of another day. The second monk, however, absolutely appalled at the gruesome sight before him, courageously declared that Dracula was a madman who would ultimately burn in hell. This infuriated Dracula, and the monk was immediately impaled in the courtyard of death.

Words misspoken in Dracula's presence often resulted in death. On the other hand, clever dialogue could preserve one's life, as witnessed in the following account:

A Polish nobleman, Benedict de Boithor, acting as ambassador of Matthias Corvinus, the king of Hungary, dined with Dracula in his castle in Tirgoviste. Impaled bodies, dead and alive, littered the dining hall, and a noxious, heavy stench hung in the air while the moans of the dying echoed off the cold castle walls. Fearing for his life, Boithor said nothing about the death around him.

After dinner, Dracula ordered his servants to place a golden stake in front of Boithor. Dracula smiled and asked,

"Tell me, why do you think I had this stake placed in front of you?"

"It seems as if some great man has angered you, and you wish to give him an honorable death," Boithor bravely replied.

"This is true," said Dracula, sliding his hand up and down the golden stake. "You speak for the great King Matthias. Thus, I shall honor you with this stake."

Boithor bowed and said, "Sir, if I have done something worthy of death, then so be it. You are a noble ruler and would not be responsible for my death. I would."

Dracula slapped his leg and laughed. "You offered the best possible answer. Had you not done so, I would have immediately impaled you! You are a true diplomat." Then Dracula honored Boithor and presented many gifts to him.[8]

German Saxons had successfully settled in Transylvania prior to Dracula's reign. The merchants were quite successful and posed a threat to the commerce of Valahia and surrounding provinces. Convinced that the monopolies established by the German merchants hindered the development of Valahian industry, Dracula initially tried to use diplomacy to negotiate trade agreements that would allow him to control the dominance of German Saxons. However, when diplomatic efforts failed, Dracula turned to violence as his chief form of negotiation. He crossed the border into Transylvania and conducted devastating raids on the German Saxons in 1457, 1459, and 1460.

---

[8] From *Dracula: Prince of Many Faces* (Published in 1989)

In the winter of 1459, Dracula and his soldiers slipped into Transylvania and conducted a horrific attack on the main suburb of Brasov. They burned the entire suburb to the ground, then impaled hundreds of men, women, and children on a nearby hill. When the smoke cleared, Dracula set up a table on the hill and dined among his hideous handiwork. He ordered butchers to cut the limbs off the bodies of many of his captives. Enjoying the anguish of his dying captives, Dracula dipped his hands in their blood and celebrated. A boyar who attended the feast held his nose and gagged because he couldn't stand the coppery, salty smell of blood that hung thick in the air. Dracula immediately impaled the boyar with an extra-long stake and sarcastically quipped, "You live up there yonder, where the stench cannot reach you."[9]

It is estimated that Dracula impaled somewhere between 2,000 and 3,000 victims during his six-year rule. Impalement was definitely his favorite means of punishment; however, he did resort to other grisly forms of torture that added to his reputation as a bloodthirsty prince. Niccoló Modrussa reported Dracula's atrocities to Pope Pius II:

He killed some by breaking them under the wheels of carts; others, stripped of their clothes, were skinned alive up to their entrails; others placed upon stakes or roasted on red-hot coals placed under them; others punctured with stakes piercing their heads, their breasts, their buttocks and

---

[9] From *In Search of Dracula: The History of Dracula and Vampires* (Published in 1994)

the middle of their entrails, with the stake emerging from their mouths; in order that no form of cruelty be missing, he stuck stakes in both the mother's breasts and thrust their babies on them. Finally, he killed others in various ferocious ways, torturing them with many kinds of instruments, such as the atrocious cruelties of the most frightful tyrant could devise.[10]

Bearing all this in mind, it comes as no surprise that Dracula would become the topic of nightmares and horror stories that would soon spread across Europe, and before long, he became known as Vlad the Impaler.

---

[10] From *In Search of Dracula: The History of Dracula and Vampires* (Published in 1994)

The Impaler vs. The Conqueror

A huge problem was developing to the southeast of Valahia: the relentless advancement of the Ottoman Turks. Dracula was certain that the day would come when Valahia would have to go to war against the Turks, and there was no way his small country could carry on two wars. Thus, in October of 1460, he struck a peace agreement with the German Saxons of Transylvania. Not only did he wish to avoid the possibility of attacks from the Saxons, but he also hoped to gain their support in his upcoming campaign against the Turks, who were led by the powerful Sultan Mehmed II, The Conqueror.

Dracula had grown up with Mehmed, and he knew the sultan wanted only one thing: the entire world! Mehmed believed the key to opening the door to the Western world was the conquering of Valahia, so he began organizing a campaign to that end. He was also annoyed because Valahia had not paid its tribute, a tax in exchange for peace, over a three-year period. Thus, Mehmed wanted to place a new prince on Valahia's throne, Radu the Handsome. In spite of the fact that Radu was his little brother, Dracula vowed in his heart that he would do whatever was necessary to save his beloved homeland and prevent his disloyal brother from taking the throne that he felt was rightfully his.

Mehmed decided that the best way to penetrate Europe was to gain control of the Danube River, an important route of transportation that stretched from the heart of Germany to the Black Sea. Mehmed mobilized troops and systematically captured towns and forts along the river from the Black Sea to Valahia.

Hoping to trap Dracula, Mehmed invited the Valahian prince to Giurgiu on the premise that he was ready to negotiate. Mehmed instructed his envoys and accompanying Turkish soldiers to ambush and kidnap Dracula outside the island fortress. But Dracula outsmarted his enemies, captured them, and impaled them outside of Tirgoviste. This daring act by Dracula was most certainly a declaration of war.

During the winter of 1461-62, Dracula launched surprise attacks on Turkish posts along the Danube and boldly began the Turkish-Valahian war. Dracula's soldiers ravaged ports and burned Turkish forts as they worked their way downriver. The Turks had little chance of defending their posts against such a vicious onslaught, and within two weeks, Dracula's army reached the Black Sea and controlled the Danube.

On February 11, 1462, Dracula bragged to King Matthias about his exploits:

I have killed men and women, old and young, who lived at Oblucitza and Novoselo, where the Danube flows into the sea, up to Rahova, which is located near Chilia, from the lower Danube up to such places as Saomovit and Ghighen. We killed 23,884 Turks and Bulgars without counting those whom we burned in homes or whose heads were not cut by our soldiers...Thus, Your Highness must know that I have broken peace with him [the sultan].[11]

Dracula's remarkable victory over the Turks was a slap in Mehmed's face. The defeat was too much for Mehmed to bear, and humiliation provoked him to launch a full-scale attack on Valahia. On May 17, 1462, Mehmed departed from Constantinople with 100,000 soldiers and set out for revenge. He had two goals in mind: He wished to punish Dracula for his brazen campaign along the Danube, and he also planned to make Valahia into a Turkish province.

On the night of June 4, 1462, the Turks closed in on Valahian soil. They hijacked seventy fishing barges, crossed the Danube, and landed at the outpost of Turnu. Mehmed and Radu, Dracula's little brother, planned to sail up the Olt River and capture Tirgoviste.

Dracula was caught off guard by the Turkish landing at Turnu, and he and his army, camped several miles away, were unable to do anything to halt the nighttime crossing of the Turks into Valahia. Not only was Dracula surprised by the Turks, but he was also at an extreme disadvantage; his army, consisting mostly of peasant men, was sorely outnumbered, three to one. Nonetheless, morale was high

---

[11] From *Dracula: Prince of Many Faces* (Published in 1989)

among Dracula's forces as they prepared to defend their homeland.

Realizing that they could not match the Turkish troops in numbers, Dracula decided to use a shrewd battle tactic, strategic retreat. Dracula intended to draw the Turks deep into Valahia, where he could use the broad plains, soggy marshes, dense forests, and rugged mountains to his advantage. He ordered his troops to retreat northward and used yet another combat technique to their advantage, the scorched-earth tactic.

As Dracula's army retreated, they left a trail of devastation in their wake, going so far as to burn and destroy their own villages and cities. Boyars, peasants, and townspeople either joined the retreating forces or fled into the mountains. The retreating army also poisoned wells, burned crops, and killed any livestock they could not take with them or herd into the surrounding mountains. Soldiers dug large pits and covered them with tree limbs, leaves, and dirt in hopes of trapping camels, horses, and men. They also built dams on small streams with the sole purpose of creating bogs that would prevent the Turks from moving their heavy cannons northward.

Mother Nature sided with the Valahians, and that further complicated matters for the Turks. The summer of 1462 was very hot, and the blazing sun beat down on the Turks as they advanced through Valahia's newly created desert. It was so hot that the Turkish armor was too hot to wear or touch. After advancing for seven days, Turkish forces found not one human or animal and nothing to eat or drink.

Dracula was a master warrior and knew the terrain of Valahia like the back of his hand. When least expected, his cavalry would strike, then disappear into the countryside before the Turks could properly defend themselves or mount a counterattack. Small bands of Turks, separated from the main force and searching for food, felt the full brunt of Dracula's hit-and-run guerrilla tactics, and most were slaughtered or impaled on the spot.

Dracula added another tactic to his bag of tricks, germ warfare. He disguised Valahia's diseased as Turks and sent them to mingle with the enemy. If one of Valahia's diseased contaminated a Turk with leprosy, the plague, or another deadly affliction, he or she was richly rewarded by Dracula.

Morale among the Turkish troops diminished with each passing day. Dracula's ingenious war tactics took a heavy toll on the their physical and mental health, but they pressed on for Tirgoviste anyway, hoping they would soon capture Dracula and end the living nightmare they found themselves in.

On June 17, 1462, the Turks were camped in the foothills of the Carpathian Mountains, just outside of Tirgoviste. It was a typical night in the Turkish camp. Guards called to each other and reported that all was well. Soldiers laughed around campfires. The smell of roasted lamb sizzling on spits wafted through the heavy summer air. Camels grunted and horses neighed. Women of the night giggled as they entertained weary soldiers in the privacy of their tents. And the sultan slept comfortably in his gold-embroidered tent that was pitched in the middle of the camp, surrounded by hundreds of others.

Just after midnight, a strange thing happened: A chorus of hoots seemed to come from owls at several points around the camp. What the sultan's people actually heard was Dracula's call to attack. Within seconds, hundreds of men, Dracula's cavalry, swooped into the Turkish camp. The warring peasants were dressed in heavy, animal-skin vests over long white shirts tied at the waist with simple leather belts. They brandished long, heavy swords, short, curved swords, axes, sickles, hammers, and bows and arrows. The few remaining boyar followers wore armor under their long, flowing robes and fought with swords, daggers, and lances.

Screams and moans echoed throughout the camp as Dracula and his cavalry galloped in and around tents, wreaking havoc and spilling the blood of drowsy and drunken Turkish soldiers. As they approached the center of the camp, Turkish guards gathered around the sultan's tent to protect their leader.

When Dracula saw the golden tent surrounded by guards, he realized he would not yet be able to assassinate Mehmed; by that time, hundreds of Turkish soldiers had joined the battle. Fearing for his own life, Dracula ordered his cavalry to retreat, and they quickly disappeared into the surrounding foothills. Thousands of Turkish soldiers lay dead, but the surprise attack had failed. Dracula lost several hundred of his best men, and Mehmed was still alive.

After the battle, Dracula inspected his wounded soldiers. He rewarded those who had wounds on the front of their bodies and impaled those who'd been wounded in the back; he had no tolerance for anyone who ran away during battle. Observing one impalement Dracula spat on the ground and proclaimed, "You are not a man but a woman."[12]

A few days later, the Turks reached Tirgoviste. Heavy smoke poured out of the city, and the gates lay open. Upon entering, the Turks found very little: no men, no cattle, no food, and no water. The city had been stripped of all valuables, and the wells had been poisoned. The sultan had no choice but to press on.

About sixty miles north of Tirgoviste, the Turks topped a hill and were greeted with a grisly sight: a forest of impaled bodies. About 1,000 Turkish captives, including men, women, and children, were hanging from stakes in a narrow gorge about a mile long. Ravens were shamelessly feasting on the mutilated, rotting bodies that had been hanging for months, and the stench of death hung heavy in the hot summer air. Chalcondyles, a Greek historian, reported that the sultan proclaimed that he could not take the land of a man who would do such things. Discouraged and frightened by what he saw, Mehmed immediately ordered the retreat of his troops.

---

[12] From *Dracula: Prince of Many Faces* (Published in 1989)

Even though Mehmed had once again been humiliated by Dracula, he still refused to give up on the Ottoman cause. Before returning home, Mehmed made what turned out to be an extremely wise decision: He left Radu the Handsome in charge of a small band of Turkish soldiers. Mehmed instructed Radu to gain a foothold in Valahia by securing the support of boyars, townspeople, and peasants. Mehmed realized that if Dracula could not be defeated by external forces, perhaps they could unseat him from within.

Rather than exercising force, Radu attempted to gain the support of the Valahians through diplomacy. Chalcondyles wrote of Radu's appeal to the Valahian people:

I am aware of the mighty forces that the sultan controls, which, sooner or later, he will use to lay waste what remains of your country. If we continue to oppose him, we shall be despoiled of all that is left to us. Why do you not reach an agreement with Sultan Mehmed? Only then will you have peace in the land and in your homes. Are you aware that there are no cattle, no horses, no farm animals, no food left in this country? Surely you have borne such sufferings long enough because of my brother, because you were loyal to this man who was responsible for more suffering than any other prince.[13]

Radu's inclination toward diplomacy began to gain the interest and support of the Valahians. Many people realized that the Ottoman Empire was still very strong and shouldn't be tested again. Most citizens were simply tired of

---

[13] From *Dracula: Prince of Many Faces* (Published in 1989)

Dracula's barbaric reign, and they were ready for a change in leadership. Six years of terror had caused the people of Valahia, rich and poor alike, to reach their limits.

By the end of the summer, Dracula's army had faded away. The boyars took up ranks with Radu, and the peasants slipped away into the mountains. Only a few loyal bodyguards and soldiers remained by Dracula's side. The situation looked very bleak for Dracula, as Radu controlled the plains and several large cities in Valahia. Desperation set in, and Dracula fled to his castle.

The Fall of Castle Dracula-Poenari

Radu and his forces pursued Dracula along the Arges River but could not capture him before he took refuge behind his thick castle walls. When they reached the village of Poenari, Radu established a small camp on a high bluff near the castle. A handful of soldiers set up cannons and aimed them at Castle Dracula-Poenari. Radu and the remaining soldiers scrambled down the bluff and set up another camp on the Arges River. Standing at the foot of the steep mountain Castle Dracula-Poenari sat upon, Radu signaled for the cannons to open fire. After several rounds, Radu concluded that the castle walls were too thick to sustain serious damage, so he summoned his soldiers and outlined a plan to seize the castle and capture Dracula the next morning.

Unbeknownst to Radu, a Romanian who had been enslaved by the Turks many years before overheard their plans. The slave, a distant relative of Dracula's, decided to warn the prince out of loyalty to his family. Under the cover of night, the slave climbed to the top of Poenari Hill and surveyed the castle. The castle was dark, except for one opening in the main tower, which flickered with dim yellow candlelight. The slave attached a warning message to an arrow, took careful aim with his bow, and let the arrow fly.

The arrow sailed through the opening and extinguished the lone candle in the room. Seconds later, light flickered through the opening once again, and the slave knew his mission had been completed successfully.

The arrow had sailed into Dracula's room as his wife was preparing to sleep. After re-lighting the candle, she read the message, then rushed down the winding staircase and found her husband in the courtyard. She showed him the message, then took Dracula's hands as a lone tear trickled down her cheek. She told him she would rather have her body eaten by the fish in the river than be captured by the Turks. Then she ran away from Dracula and raced up the staircase to the top of the tower. Before anyone could do anything, she climbed through an opening, jumped out into the empty darkness, and fell hundreds of feet to her death in the rock-strewn river.

Being hard of heart, Dracula wasted no time mourning his wife's death. He knew he had to act quickly to save his own life, so he immediately sent for help from the nearby shepherd village of Arefu. Within the hour, help arrived in the form of seven brothers of the Dobrin family. The brothers entered the courtyard, bowed before Dracula, and bravely offered their services. After much discussion, it was decided that the best course of action would be for the brothers to help Dracula escape over the Carpathian Mountains into Transylvania, which was controlled by Hungary.

Dracula needed their help because crossing the rugged mountains would be a treacherous ordeal. No mountain roads or passes existed at that time, and steep cliffs, deep gorges, loose rocks, rushing streams, and even ice and snow made the mountain summits nearly impassable. The Dobrins had intimate knowledge of the surrounding highlands, and he knew if anyone could guide him to safety, it would be them. Even with their help, though, the trek would be dangerous.

Dracula felt that fleeing to Transylvania would be a smart move on his part, because it was rumored that King Matthias had recently left Budapest and was en route to Brasov. Dracula hoped to meet with Matthias so he could convince him to form an alliance. With the support of the Hungarians, Dracula believed he could retake Valahia from Radu.

A couple hours before dawn, Dracula, his young son, twelve trusted guards, and five of the Dobrin brothers departed the castle and silently worked their way down the steep mountainside, until they arrived at a cave on the banks of the river, just a mile north of the Turkish camp. Dracula and his entourage paced nervously in the dank cave and talked in hushed whispers as they waited for horses to be brought from Arefu. A short while later, the horses arrived, and the Dobrin brothers led Dracula, his son (who was tied to Dracula's saddle), and his guards up the mountainside under the cover of darkness. The Dobrins knew exactly what they were doing; they had even gone as far as to shod the horses backward to confuse the Turks!

Castle cannons fired into the valley below to throw off the Turks as Dracula's party fled up the treacherous peak. The Turks returned the favor and pounded the castle with cannon fire of their own. The relentless booming startled Dracula's horse, causing the animal to buck and stumble over some loose rock. Dracula's son came loose from the saddle and toppled to the ground. In the ensuing panic and commotion, the boy was lost, but Dracula pressed onward without searching for the boy; the threat of the nearby Turks was far more painful for him than the loss of his son, and he gladly gave up his child's life to preserve his own.

Several days later, the fleeing party safely reached the summit of the mountains. Behind them lay Castle Dracula-Poenari, most likely in the hands of Radu and the Turks, and before them lay Brasov, where it was hoped that the Hungarians were waiting to help Dracula.

Dracula gathered the Dobrin brothers and asked them how he could pay them back for saving his life. They replied that they wanted nothing; they had faithfully and bravely served their country, and that was enough. But Dracula insisted that they be rewarded, so he asked them if they wanted money or land. The brothers finally consented and said land would be sufficient. On the skin of a rabbit, Dracula wrote an order granting the Dobrins ownership of all the mountains as far as they could see, and he also specified that the land could never be taken away by anyone. Then he turned his back on them and led his twelve guards down the mountain slopes, toward Brasov.

Double-Crossed

King Matthias arrived in Brasov in November of 1462. Dracula settled in the Scheii district, just outside the city walls, so he could flee quickly if the need arose. For five weeks, Matthias and Dracula met in the town hall and discussed their precarious situation. Each day, Dracula tried to persuade Matthias that a joint crusade was their only chance to take Valahia back from Radu and the Turks. Finally, Matthias agreed with Dracula, and a small crusade was organized; however, the king's plans were much different than those of the former prince of Valahia.

Matthias gave Dracula a small band of soldiers, to be co-commanded by Ján Jiskra, a former Slovakian mercenary, and sent them off toward Valahia with the understanding that full Hungarian support would follow. On December 5, Dracula and Jiskra reached Königstein Fort, which straddled the Transylvanian-Valahian territory along the Bran-Rucar Pass.

The small fort, perched on the edge of a 1,000-foot cliff, stood watch over the pass. The imposing cliff was a natural barrier, too steep and treacherous for even the most steady-footed to climb; however, it was essential that Dracula and Jiskra reach the pass below. The co-leaders started lowering soldiers, horses, wagons, and supplies down the precipice via rope and pulley. The process was slow and dangerous, but by early afternoon of the next day, all of Dracula's soldiers had been lowered. They milled around, staring up at the fort, waiting for their leader to follow. As Dracula tied a rope around his waist, Jiskra and a couple of his soldiers grabbed Dracula, tied him up, and arrested him. Down below, Dracula's soldiers ranted and raved when they realized what had happened, but there was nothing they could do to rescue their beloved leader.

Dracula protested and demanded an explanation. Jiskra, who had never liked Dracula in the first place, forced his prisoner into a wagon and gruffly explained that the operation had been staged under direct orders by King Matthias. The king's secret plan was successful, and for the first time in his life, Dracula had been double-crossed.

Matthias arrested Dracula because he wanted him out of the way. Dracula's desire to regain his throne, with the help of Hungary, had never been seriously entertained by Matthias. Prior to Dracula's arrest, Matthias had officially recognized Radu the Handsome as prince of Valahia, and he'd also signed a secret five-year peace treaty with Sultan Mehmed II. Matthias had earlier received 40,000 gold ducats from Pope Pius II to aid Dracula in a campaign against the Turks, but the money had been spent elsewhere, because Matthias had no intention of ever helping Dracula.

By Christmas, Dracula was imprisoned in Buda, the capital of Hungary, but his imprisonment posed a serious problem for Matthias. In the eyes of many other European leaders, Dracula was considered a hero. He had, after all, singlehandedly defeated Mehmed for the Christian cause and had postponed the advance of the Ottomans, at least for the time being. Numerous Europeans wanted to know why the brave Christian crusader had been unjustly imprisoned.

King Matthias accounted for his extreme action by producing three letters, allegedly written by Dracula on November 7, 1462, sent from Rothel and apparently bearing Dracula's signature. One was addressed to Sultan Mehmed II, one to a renegade named Mahmud, and the last to Prince Stephen of Moldavia. The content of the letters suggested that Dracula had abandoned the Christian cause and was eager to help Mehmed conquer Transylvania and Hungary. The letter to Mehmed even stated that Dracula would help abduct King Matthias if necessary.

European leaders were suspicious of Matthias and his letters. They wondered how it could be possible that Dracula would make such a turnabout and support the sultan after recently crusading against him. There was even suspicion that the letters were forgeries, and it was questionable whether or not a place named Rothel even existed. The whole affair turned into an embarrassing situation for Matthias.

Regardless, Dracula remained in Hungarian hands and was moved twenty miles north of Buda to Matthias' impressive summer castle in Visegrád, where he was held in custody from 1462 through 1474. The castle, sitting high above the Danube, overlooked beautiful forested hillsides full of deer, wild boar, and other game.

Dracula was held under house arrest in Visegrád for twelve years, but he was not a prisoner, in the real sense of the word. He did not spend his Visegrád years in a dark, damp dungeon. His life was fairly comfortable, but he had little freedom and was always under the watchful eye of a guard. Basically, Dracula was a pawn in a diplomatic chess game. Matthias held him as a hostage to intimidate the Turks. If Mehmed ever broke their treaty, Matthias would be obliged to release and support Vlad the Impaler in a new crusade against the Turks.

Freedom

Basarab Laiota, a member of the Danesti family, captured Valahia's throne from Radu the Handsome in November of 1473. Within weeks, Radu staged a comeback, and the two battled throughout the following year for control of the throne. The contest did not come to an end until Radu died early in 1475.

Basarab immediately aligned himself with the Turks, which alienated him from the Hungarians. As far as King Matthias was concerned, Basarab was untrustworthy and a threat to the European Empire. Matthias knew Basarab had to be dealt with, and he was sure the perfect man for the job was Dracula, who would most certainly be willing and able. Strangely enough, Matthias offered his support to Dracula under one condition: He had to marry into the king's family. To uphold his end of the bargain, Dracula married Ilona Szilágy, a cousin of Matthias, and became a member of the royal family. Now a free man, Dracula left Visegrád, bypassed Buda, and settled down across the Danube River in Pest, where he and his family lived a prosperous life in a stately mansion.

During the summer of 1476, King Matthias granted his full support to organize a campaign to take Valahia from Basarab, a joint effort that would be led by Dracula,

Stephen Báthory (a prominent Hungarian), and Vuk Brankovic (a Serbian tyrant). Stephen the Great of Moldavia, Dracula's cousin, would also have a hand in the maneuvers. Hungarian, Transylvanian, Moldavian, Serbian, and Valahian troops would be involved in the crusade.

Unfortunately, the Valahian offensive had to be postponed for a while. The Turks had overrun Moldavia, a move that greatly threatened Dracula's Valahian campaign. Remembering the oath he'd made to Stephen many years before, Dracula headed northeast, hoping to help his own flesh and blood. The two cousins met in mid-August at the Oituz Pass on the Transylvanian border. They quickly combined their troops and chased the Turks, crushing them at the Siret River and opening the doors for the Valahian campaign to begin.

In early November, Basarab and his army of 18,000 soldiers confronted the combined forces of Báthory and Dracula near the town of Rucar. A fierce battle commenced, and when it was over, Basarab and his remaining forces fled for safety. Báthory and Dracula raised their bloody swords above their heads and proclaimed victory as they surveyed the battleground littered with bodies. The battle was costly for both armies, and 10,000 soldiers from each side lay dead. In the meantime, while Báthory and Dracula celebrated their victory, Stephen the Great captured northeastern Valahia from the Turks, pumping additional momentum into the campaign.

By November 8, Tirgoviste, the capital city, was back in Dracula's control. With their spirits high, Dracula and

Stephen met in Tirgoviste and swore, once again, that they would support each other forever, even unto death. They also swore that they would continue their crusade until the Ottomans were no longer a threat to Christian Europe.

The remaining cities, towns, and villages of Valahia fell to Dracula like dominoes, and on November 26, in the village of Curtea de Arges, Dracula became the prince of Valahia once again. The ceremony was small, and there were few supporters in attendance because Dracula was hated by many, particularly the Saxons, the boyars, Basarab, and the Turks.

Dracula realized that many wished him dead and that his life was in jeopardy. Thus, he did not ask his family to join him in Bucharest, the new seat of the government. He left them in Transylvania so they would not be exposed to the risks he faced. To make matters even more ominous for him, Báthory and Stephen pulled out of Valahia, leaving Dracula in Bucharest, with little support. He ruled Valahia once again, but no one knew how long that would last.

Another Assassination

Dracula recognized that his future was uncertain, that his government and his life could be toppled at any time. This grim knowledge led him to prepare for the inevitable. He loaded cast-iron barrels with gold, silver, and jewels, wealth that would be needed if a crisis situation developed. Local peasants, honoring Dracula's orders, damned and diverted the course of the Dîmbovita River. They buried the barrels in the empty riverbed, then destroyed the dam; when the river began to flow again, it concealed Dracula's treasures. Hoping to preserve the secret of where his riches lay buried, Dracula immediately impaled the peasants who had served him so well.

Meanwhile, Basarab proceeded to the Danube and drafted the help of several Turkish commanders and their troops. Basarab had one goal in mind: to assassinate Dracula as soon as possible. Still, he knew it would be nearly impossible to get close to Dracula.

He and the Turkish commanders devised a plan that they hoped would ensure the death of Dracula. In early December, they hired an undercover assassin and sent him into Dracula's camp. The assassin's initial responsibility was to act as a servant and gain his trust, but in reality, he was tasked with murdering the leader of Valahia.

Near the end of December, Basarab and his 4,000 Turkish troops attacked Dracula in the frost-covered marshes near the island monastery of Snagov. Dracula's force of 2,000 men, including 200 Moldavian bodyguards, rallied around their leader and began slaughtering the enemy with reckless abandon. Battle cries pierced the cold winter air, and the repulsive smell of blood, guts, sweat, and death blanketed the battlefield. Steam rose off the bodies that littered the marshes, and a lone vulture circled above the skirmish, watching and waiting.

Dracula climbed a nearby hill for the vulture's view of the furious battle. Within minutes, a handful of servants, including the undercover assassin, joined him to see if they could be of assistance. Dracula, lost in thought, ignored the servants and stared at the carnage before him. Seizing the moment, the assassin lunged at Dracula and shoved a spear in his back. Dracula screamed in rage as a dozen Turkish soldiers quickly clambered up the hill to assist the assassin. Dracula attacked the band of warriors like a madman. Five Turks fell to Dracula's sword, but more surrounded him, and within minutes, his spear-riddled body crumpled to the ground in a heap.

News of Dracula's death quickly spread through the ranks, and the battle came to a halt. Dracula's remaining soldiers immediately fled the battlefield and disappeared into the nearby forest. Basarab and a small group of Turks climbed the hill and stared in silence at the lifeless body of Vlad the Impaler, finding it difficult to believe that the man was really dead. The assassin stepped forward, drew his sword, cut Dracula's head off, and held it high in the air, proclaiming that he would personally deliver the head of Vlad the Impaler to the sultan himself.

Later that night, monks gathered the headless body from the foggy, frozen marsh and buried it in a crypt at the nearby monastery on the island of Snagov. And Dracula's bloody reign of terror was over at the age of forty-five.

Epilogue

Once Again: Who Was Dracula?

To most people, Dracula was a bloodsucking night demon who terrorized the living. To many Romanians, he was a hero who gave his life for his country. To others, he was one of the cruelest villains of all time. Was he a bloodsucker, a hero, or a villain? Perhaps he was all three.

About the Author

Ken Derby is a slightly famous author, monkey trainer, twelve-minute rock star, five-minute TV star, two-minute movie star, fisherman, and former CIA operative (okay ... not really). When he isn't teaching or writing, he might be found reading, working out, biking, or rooting for the Denver Broncos. Visit him at www.kenderby.com.

A Note From the Author ...

Dear Reader,

If you thought this book totally rocked, I'd be eternally grateful if you posted a review on Amazon. It would also be cool if you shared your thoughts about this book on Facebook, Twitter, Goodreads, and your other social networks.

All the best,
Ken

The European and Ottoman (Turkish) Empires During Dracula's Time

DRACULA'S ROMANIA

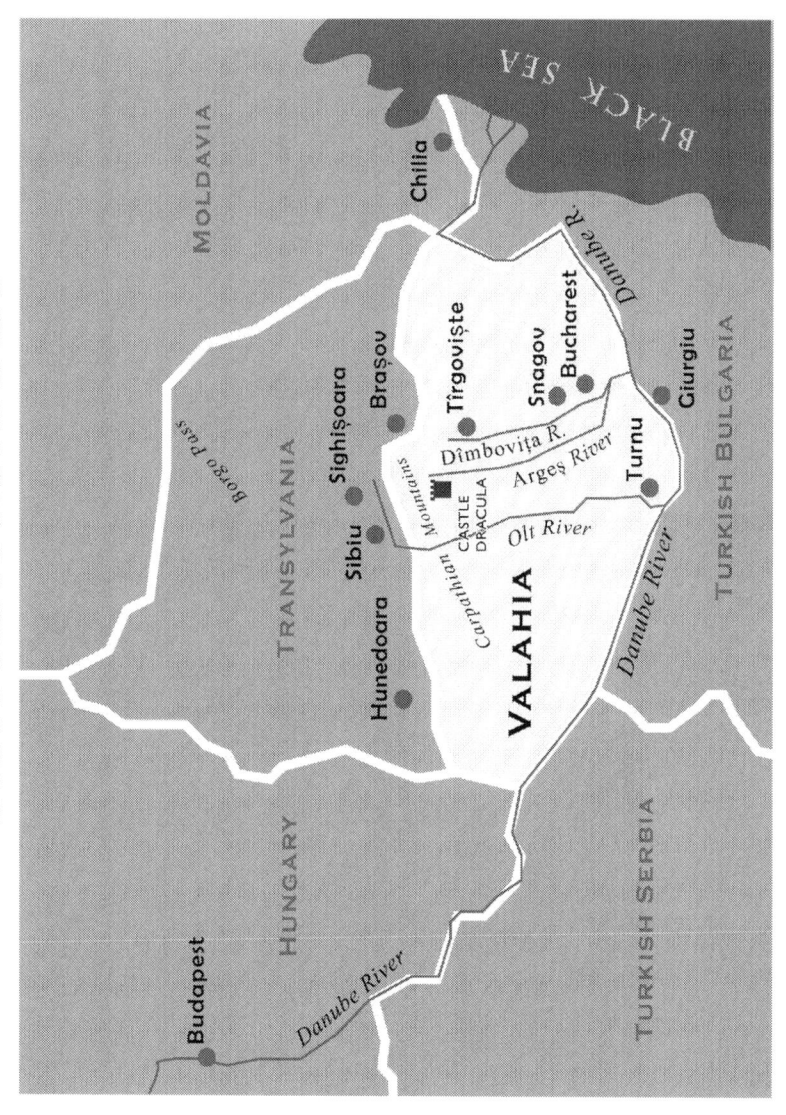

Glossary of Important Historical Figures

Aldea, Alexandru—Dracul's half-brother and Prince of Valahia from 1431-36

Báthory, Stephen—a prominent Hungarian and governor of Transylvania from 1479 until his death in 1493

Boithor, Benedict de—Polish nobleman and ambassador of King Matthias

Brankovic, Vuk—a Serbian tyrant

Chalcondyles—a Greek historian

Dobrin Brothers—shepherds from the village of Arefu

Dracul, Vlad—father of Dracula and prince of Valahia from 1436-42

Dracula, Vlad—son of Dracul and prince of Valahia from October to November 1448, from 1456-62, and from November to December 1476

Hunyadi, John—viceroy of Hungary and governor of Transylvania from 1446-53

Jiskra, Ján—a Slovakian mercenary

Laiota, Basarab—a member of the Danesti family and prince of Valahia from 1473-76

Matthias Corvinus—King of Hungary from 1458-90; also known as King Matthias

Mehmed II—son of Murad II and sultan of the Ottoman Empire from 1444-46 and 1451-81

Mircea—Dracula's older brother and prince of Valahia from 1442-43

Modrussa, Niccolò—papal legate to Buda

Murad II—father of Mehmed II and sultan of the Ottoman Empire from 1421-51

Pius II, Pope—pontificate from 1458-64

Radu the Handsome—Dracula's younger brother and prince of Valahia from 1462-73 and in 1475

Sigismund of Luxembourg—king of Luxembourg from 1387-1437; also the Holy Roman Emperor from 1411-33

and king of Bohemia in 1420; also known as King or Emperor Sigismund

Stephen the Great—cousin of Dracula and prince of Moldavia from 1457-1504

Szilágy, Ilona—cousin of King Matthias and second wife of Dracula

Vladislav II—a member of the Danesti family and prince of Valahia from 1447 till October 1448 and then from December 1448-1456

Research Sources

Bunson, Matthew. *The Vampire Encyclopedia*. New York: Crown, 1993.

Florescu, Radu. R., and Raymond T. McNally. *Dracula, Prince of Many Faces*. Boston: Little Brown, 1989.

Florescu, Radu. R., and Raymond T. McNally. *In Search of Dracula: The History of Dracula and Vampires*. New York: Houghton Mifflin, 1994.

Guiley, Rosemary Ellen. *The Complete Vampire Companion*. New York: Macmillan, 1994.

Melton, J. Gordon. *The Vampire Book*. Detroit: Visible Ink Press, 1994.

Miller, Elizabeth. *Reflections on Dracula: Ten Essays*. White Rock, Canada: Transylvania Press, 1997.

Stoker, Bram. *Dracula*. Westminster, U.K.: Constable, 1897

Links

Visit the Transylvanian Society of Dracula at the following websites.

Wikipedia
http://en.wikipedia.org/wiki/Transylvanian_Society_of_Dracula

Transylvanian Society of Dracula: Canadian Chapter
http://blooferland.com/tsd.html

Transylvanian Society of Dracula at Vampire Junction
http://www.afn.org/~vampires/tsd.html

Transylvanian Society of Dracula: United Kingdom Chapter
https://www.facebook.com/transylvaniansocietyofdracula

Transylvanian Society of Dracula: Latest News
http://www.mysteriousjourneys.com/dracula_tours/latest_news/

Transylvanian Society of Dracula at Flickr
http://www.flickr.com/groups/transylvaniansocietyofdracula/

Dracula's Homepage (maintained by Dr. Elizabeth Miller)
http://www.ucs.mun.ca/~emiller/

Other Books by Ken Derby

The Top 10 Ways to Ruin the First Day of School

An International Reading Association and Children's Book Council "Children's Choices" Honor Book

An Alabama "Children's Choice Book Award Program" Winner

"Nonstop wacky action." – School Library Journal

"A quick, fun read that will appeal to would-be show-offs everywhere." – Booklist

"This very funny, very silly book is filled with kids, teachers and parents who will make you laugh - when you're not chuckling about Tony's latest antics." – The Washington Post

Anthony Madison, a.k.a. Tony Baloney, can't get enough of the Late Show with David Letterman. He loves the Late Show and will stop at nothing to get himself on the program. But to get from Kansas City to New York City, he'll have to pull out all the stops. With his own brand of Top Ten lists, and stunts that range from photocopying his hinder to taking to the field in a bear suit at a professional football game, Tony takes the NFL, MTV, New York City, the Hells Angels, his teacher, friends, family, and readers on an uproarious ride to remember.

Available at Amazon and other online bookstores.

Harley P. Davidsun's Loony Bin

"Don't read this book if you are nervous about falling off a chair or out of bed when you are reading. This is a very funny story and sure to be a big hit!" – JOHANNA HURWITZ, award-winning author of more than sixty popular books for children

Harley Patrick Davidsun, the zany biker/rocker/teacher dude from *The Top 10 Ways to Ruin the First Day of School*, is back! And his classroom is not what one would call "traditional." He's nicknamed it "The Fourth Grade Loony Bin," and that's exactly what it is, especially when he pits the boys against the girls in a contest to win a ride on his chopped motorcycle. Humorous events – ranging from a flatulence test to Kiss-A-Mania – mean you'll never know what's going to happen next. So step into the Loony Bin and find out who wins the wacky contest. You'll be glad you went along for the ride!

WARNING! Many things in this story are totally outrageous, and adults will say that such things could never happen in real life. But what do they know? Maybe somewhere, in some distant school, there really is a teacher like Harley P. Davidsun. At least, let's hope so.

Available at Amazon and other online bookstores.

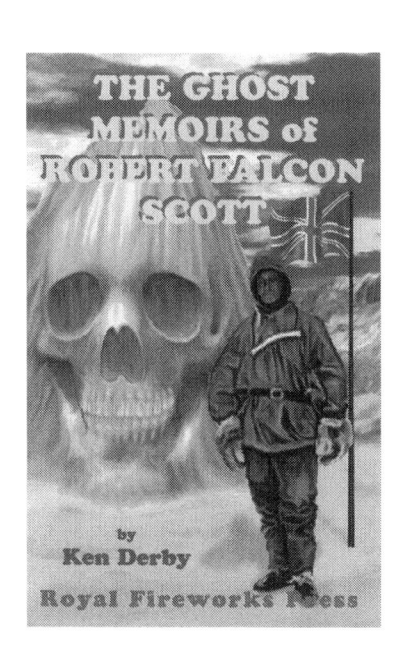

The Ghost Memoirs of Robert Falcon Scott

One never knows what's going to pop up on their monitor when online. Ken Derby, the author, was surfing cyberspace when he was contacted – via his computer – by the ghost of Robert Falcon Scott, famed British polar explorer. *The Ghost Memoirs of Robert Falcon Scott* is the result of a supernatural exchange in which Scott shares his story of how he became a relentless explorer with one goal in mind: the South Pole. Scott finally reached his goal, but met a tragic death in Antarctica in 1912. This story is comprised of transcripts of e-mail conversations between Scott and the author as well as Scott's first-person account of his life. The book includes two maps, a glossary of terms, a glossary of places, and a bibliography.

Available online at Royal Fireworks Press and at Amazon.

The Mystery of King Tutankhamun

During Egypt's Eighteenth Dynasty, the Valley of the Kings was used as a royal graveyard. Over the next 3000 years, all but three tombs were discovered in that hot, barren valley. By the early 1900s, most archaeologists believed the three missing royal burial sites were located somewhere else. One of those tombs belonged to Tutankhamun, Egypt's boy king.

However, Howard Carter, an archeologist, and George Herbert, a classic English aristocrat, believed differently. The two met for the first time in 1909 and discovered that they had something in common: a strong desire to find the location of Tutankhamun's tomb. They formed an alliance and set their sights on this seemingly unattainable goal.

With imagined dialogue, Ken Derby reveals the true-life adventure story of Howard Carter, his discovery of King Tutankhamun's tomb, his attempts to unravel the mysteries surrounding this ancient Egyptian child king, and the puzzling "curses" that seemed to follow many involved with the tomb's discovery.

Available at Amazon and other online bookstores.

Printed in Great Britain
by Amazon